AR PTS: 2.0

GREAT CITIES OF THE WORLD

BERLIN

NICOLA BARBER

WORLD ALMANAC® LIBRARY

Please visit our web site at: www.worldalmanaclibrary.com
For a free color catalog describing World Almanac® Library's list of high-quality books
and multimedia programs, call 1-800-848-2928 (USA) or 1-800-387-3178 (Canada).
World Almanac® Library's fax: (414) 332-3567.

Library of Congress Cataloging-in-Publication Data

Barber, Nicola.
 Berlin / by Nicola Barber.
   p. cm. — (Great cities of the world)
 Includes bibliographical references and index.
 ISBN 0-8368-5043-2 (lib. bdg.)
 ISBN 0-8368-5203-6 (softcover)
 1. Berlin (Germany)—Juvenile literature. I. Title. II. Series.
 DD860.B37   2005
 943'.155—dc22   2004057827

First published in 2005 by
World Almanac® Library
330 West Olive Street, Suite 100
Milwaukee, WI 53212 USA

Copyright © 2005 by World Almanac® Library.

Produced by Discovery Books
Editors: Valerie Weber and Kathryn Walker
Series designers: Laurie Shock, Keith Williams
Designer and page production: Keith Williams
Photo researcher: Tom Humphrey
Diagrams: Keith Williams
Maps: Stefan Chabluk
World Almanac® Library editorial direction: Mark J. Sachner
World Almanac® Library editor: Gini Holland
World Almanac® Library art direction: Tammy West
World Almanac® Library graphic design: Scott M. Krall
World Almanac® Library production: Jessica Morris

Photo credits: AKG Images: pp. 8, 9, 13, 14, 15, 24, 37; Corbis/Martin Beebe: p. 32; Eye-Ubiquitous/Hugh Rooney:
pp. 4, 31; Getty Images/AFP/Michael Kappeler: p. 42; Getty Images/AFP/Kulturedesign: 21; James Davis Travel: p. 10;
James Davis Travel/Jon Hicks: p. 26; Panos/Stefan Boness: pp. 18, 20, 35, 36, 40; Panos/Visum/Carsten Koall: p. 29;
Still Pictures/Reinhard Janke: p. 17; Still Pictures/Thomas Mayer: 23; Still Pictures/Thomas Raupach: p. 7; Still Pictures/
Johann Scheibner: p. 38; Still Pictures/Otto Stadler: p. 22; Trip: p. 41; Trip/T. Bognar: cover and title page, p. 27.

**Cover caption: Berlin's most famous landmark, the Brandenburg Gate, was built in 1791 as a triumphal
entrance to the city, but while the Berlin Wall divided East and West Berlin from 1961 to 1989, the Gate
stood in no man's land and was closed off. After the demolition of the Wall, the Brandenburg Gate
became a symbol of the freedom and reunification of the city.**

Printed in Canada

1 2 3 4 5 6 7 8 9 09 08 07 06 05

Contents

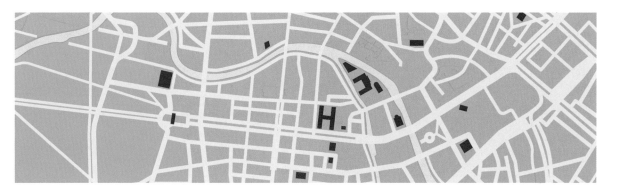

Introduction

Berlin's extraordinary history includes a time when a concrete wall split it in two parts—West Berlin and East Berlin. Berlin is still dealing with the aftermath of its years as a divided city; since the Berlin Wall came down in 1989, it has been in almost constant change. The capital city of Germany today, Berlin boasts one of the most vibrant cultural scenes in the Western world, with music, theater, opera, dance, and galleries to suit all tastes. It also has some of the most exciting modern architecture built by some of the world's best-known architects, most notably

◀ *This panoramic view over Berlin's central city area was taken from the Funkturm, the city's radio tower located in the Charlottenburg district.*

the stunning Jüdisches Museum (Jewish Museum) designed by the Polish architect Daniel Libeskind.

Although there is evidence of settlement from the Stone Age, Berlin's history proper begins with the arrival of various Germanic and Slavic tribes. The name Berlin could derive from *birl*, the Slav word for "swamp;" much of the area used to be marshland.

Berlin started life as a trading center, and that tradition continues today. Geographically, Berlin is situated at a convenient point between Eastern and Western Europe; it is now exploiting this position in its drive to improve the city's economy.

Berlin is both a city and one of the sixteen *länder* (states) that today make up the Federal Republic of Germany. Completely surrounded by the state of Brandenburg, it was both part of that state and its capital until the end of World War II in 1945, when the entire country itself split into two—East Germany and West Germany. In the years after the war, when the former Allies controlled Berlin, the capital of West Germany moved to Bonn, while the capital of East Germany was East Berlin. When the two Germanys were reunified in 1990, it was quickly confirmed that the capital of the new Germany would once again be Berlin.

Geography

Berlin lies on the northern German plains and is mainly low-lying. Some of its hills are in fact artificial, formed out of rubble cleared from the devastated city after World War II.

CITY FACTS

Berlin
Capital of the Federal Republic of Germany

Founded: 1244

Area: 343 square miles (889 square kilometers)

Population: 3,389,500

Population Density: 9,882 per sq m (3,813 per sq km)

The city lies on two rivers, the Spree and the Havel, that join in the Spandau district in western Berlin. Canals also crisscross the city. There are many lakes, most notably the Wannsee and the Tegeler See formed by the Havel in the west, and the Müggelsee, part of the Spree River network in the east. The Grunewald and the Düppler Forst are large areas of forest in the western part of the city.

Then and Now, a Bustling City

Since the reunification of East and West Berlin, Potsdamer Platz has been redeveloped to provide a center point for the new Berlin. At the beginning of the twentieth century, this square was a busy hub, full of traffic, theaters, and hotels. Destroyed during World War II, it was left abandoned during the years following

Berlin City Center

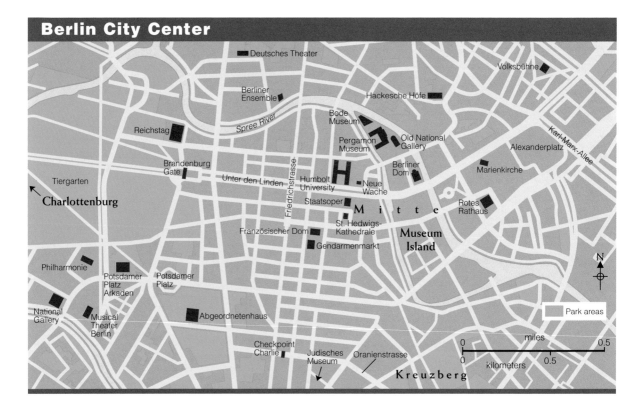

Berlin City Area

the war, because it stood right next to the Berlin Wall that divided the city. Now, however, it is the home of some of Berlin's most modern and exciting architecture.

Berlin remains a city of many separate neighborhoods, each with its own character. The historic center lies in Mitte, which includes Museum Island, an island in the Spree River with an impressive collection of museums. One of the most famous streets in Berlin, Unter den Linden, runs west from Museum Island to the Brandenburg Gate on the eastern edge of the Tiergarten. The Brandenburg Gate once marked the boundary between East and West Berlin and was a powerful symbol of the divided city during those years, while the Tiergarten, a large park in the center of Berlin, was once a royal hunting estate. Since reunification, an area north of the Tiergarten has been developed as the new government

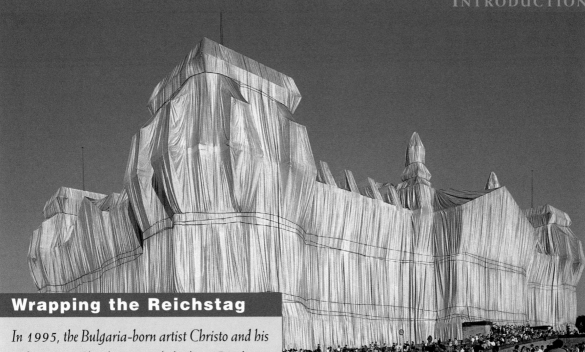

Wrapping the Reichstag

In 1995, the Bulgaria-born artist Christo and his wife Jeanne-Claude wrapped the huge Reichstag building completely in silver-colored fabric (pictured above). This artistic event lasted for two weeks. It had taken Christo many years to persuade the German authorities to allow him to do this, but the wrapping was a huge success; thousands of people came to see the Reichstag as it had never been seen before. The event also marked an important moment in Berlin's history because when the wrappings came off, the renovation of the Reichstag began according to a design by the British architect, Sir Norman Foster.

Climate

Berlin has a cool climate, with the warmest temperatures in the summer months reaching around 77° Fahrenheit (25° Celsius) and the coldest temperatures in winter dropping below –23° Fahrenheit (–5° C). The coldest months are December, January, and February, when bitter winds blowing in from Russia can also bring heavy snowfalls.

district with the home of the German parliament, the Reichstag, at its center. The areas west of the Tiergarten, Kurfürstendamm, and Charlottenburg, formed the main neighborhoods of West Berlin, while to the south Kreuzberg is home to many of the Turkish immigrants who have made Berlin their home.

"All free men, wherever they may live, are citizens of Berlin. And therefore, as a free man, I take pride in the words 'Ich bin ein Berliner.'"

—U.S. President John F. Kennedy
at West Berlin City Hall, June 26, 1963.

CHAPTER 1

History of Berlin

Archaeological discoveries show that the site occupied by present-day Berlin was settled as early as the Stone Age. Next, during the first centuries A.D., various tribes settled along the banks of the Havel and Spree Rivers, including the Germanic Semnones. By the end of the sixth century, the Semnones were forced to compete for territory with various Slavic tribes, including the Heveller and the Sprewanen. The Hevellers built forts at Spandau and Köpenick, now suburbs in northwest and southeast Berlin.

Albrecht the Bear

During the twelfth century, the Saxon Albrecht the Bear, of the Askanian family, became the first Margrave (Count) of Brandenburg. Albrecht gradually forced the Slavs to leave, and the area was resettled by people from west of the Elbe River. During the early thirteenth century, the twin settlements of Cölln (on present -day Museum Island) and Berlin grew up on opposite sides of the Spree River, halfway between the fortress towns of Spandau and Köpenick. Both towns were on important trading routes, handling mainly fish, timber,

◄ This nineteenth-century picture shows Albrecht the Bear attacking Fort Brennabor in Brandenburg in 1150. Albrecht took control of a large area of modern-day northern Germany in the twelfth century.

and rye (a type of grain). In 1307, they formed an alliance, called Berlin-Cölln, and in 1359 became part of the trading organization known as the Hanseatic League.

The Hohenzollerns

During the fourteenth century, after the death of the last Askanian ruler in 1319, rival families struggled for control of Berlin-Cölln. The arrival of Friedrich of Hohenzollern, a noble from southern Germany, brought this bitter feud to an end nearly one hundred years later. Assuming control of the area, he established his family as the rulers of Brandenburg, taking the title "Elector" of Brandenburg. The two towns began to lose their separate identities and, in 1432, were formally united as one. In 1442, work began on the first castle in Berlin-Cölln, the future Stadtschloss (City Castle) on present-day Museum Island. Despite a short-lived rebellion from 1447 to 1448 against the rule of the Hohenzollerns, by 1486, Berlin-Cölln was the capital of Brandenburg and the permanent home of the Hohenzollern family. The Hohenzollerns remained in power until 1918.

Reformation and Reconstruction

In 1517, a German monk, Martin Luther attacked many of the practices of the Roman Catholic Church, which he considered corrupt, and suggested various reforms. His action sparked a movement called the Reformation. Supporters of the

Französischer Dom, the French Cathedral

This cathedral, in Gendarmenmarkt, Friedrichstadt, was built for the French Huguenots who made their home in Berlin-Cölln in the seventeenth century. The church (pictured above) was constructed between 1701 and 1705, by which time the Huguenot community in the city included about six thousand members. The Huguenots were Protestants who followed the teachings of John Calvin. The Catholic government of France persecuted them, but in 1598, the Edict of Nantes gave the Huguenots the right to worship in some places. In 1685, King Louis XIV repealed this proclamation, and the Huguenots were expelled from France. Many came to Berlin-Cölln at the invitation of the Hohenzollern ruler.

Reformation became known as Protestants. The ideas of the Reformation reached Berlin-Cölln very quickly, and Elector Joachim II adopted the Protestant faith in 1539. However, the Thirty Years War (1618–1648), which was fought between the Catholic armies of the Holy Roman Empire and Protestant armies backed by Sweden, had a devastating effect on Berlin-Cölln. The city was sacked repeatedly, the elector and his court fled to Königsberg, northeast of Berlin (in what is now Russia), and trade collapsed. By the end of the war, the population had halved to a mere six thousand people, and a large part of the city was destroyed.

▼ *Elector Friedrich III (King Friedrich I) built Schloss Charlottenburg, intending it to be a summer palace for his wife, Sophie-Charlotte. Work began on the palace in 1695 and continued throughout the eighteenth century.*

It fell to another von Hohenzollern, Friedrich Wilhelm, the "Great Elector," who ruled from 1640 to 1688, to reconstruct the city. Friedrich Wilhelm oversaw the construction of new fortifications around the city, of a canal linking the Spree and Oder Rivers, and of three new towns—Friedrichswerder, Dorotheenstadt, and Friedrichstadt, all part of the modern-day district of Mitte. Friedrich Wilhelm also encouraged immigrants to come to the city. About fifty wealthy Jewish families came from Vienna, Austria, as well as a large number of Huguenots from France.

Capital of Prussia

In 1701, Elector Friedrich III (son of the Great Elector) raised the status of Brandenburg to a kingdom and had himself crowned as king of Brandenburg-Prussia. Friedrich was ambitious in other matters,

too; he set about making Berlin a cultural and scientific center, founding an Academy of Arts in 1696 and an Academy of Sciences in 1700. The castle was turned into a palace, and a summer palace was built at Charlottenburg, west of Berlin. His son, King Friedrich Wilhelm I, who ruled from 1713 to 1740, was very different. He became known as the Soldier-King because of his determination to build up a sizable army. He constructed another wall around Berlin—not to keep intruders out but to prevent the city's citizens from escaping their required service in the military.

Frederick the Great

The next ruler, King Friedrich II, ruled from 1740 to 1786 and was known to English-speakers as Frederick the Great. He was a military man like his father; his desire to win territory in Silesia east of Berlin led to a series of wars including the Seven Years War (1756–1763). Unlike his father, however, Frederick the Great loved the arts. He promoted Berlin as a cultural center, as well as overseeing many architectural developments in the city. By the late eighteenth century, Berlin had become an important center for German Romanticism, with philosophers, writers, artists, and scientists meeting at salons across the city.

Occupation and Industrialization

In 1806, the French troops of Emperor Napoléon Bonaparte occupied Berlin. King

The Humboldts

Berlin's oldest university was founded in 1809 by one of two remarkable brothers, Wilhelm von Humboldt, and is now named after him. The Humboldts were brought up in Berlin, where Wilhelm (1767–1835) became a statesman and lawyer. His brother Alexander (1769–1859) was a scientist and geographer. He worked as a mine inspector before setting off on several years travel to South and Central America. Alexander Humboldt used observations from his journeys to lay down the foundations of much of modern-day geography and meteorology. He later became a professor at the university in Berlin.

Friedrich Wilhelm III fled the city, and the French removed many priceless works of art and sent them back to France. King Wilhelm III's royal court returned to Berlin in 1809, and, after France received huge sums of money, the French troops finally left the city.

After the defeat of Napoléon at the Battle of Waterloo in 1815, Prussia gained territories in the Rhineland and Westphalia west of Berlin. These areas provided minerals and raw materials for the rapid growth of industry that took place during the early nineteenth century. Berlin was at the center of this industrialization, with men such as August Borsig setting up factories in the city. The first railway track, from Berlin to Potsdam, opened in 1838.

The abundance of factory jobs in Berlin attracted thousands of workers to Berlin and led to the creation of a new working class in the city.

Unification

The nineteenth century was a time of unrest in Berlin. People began to question the right of the nobility to rule; they demanded reform, including freedom of the press and a constitution. Matters came to a head in 1848, the year of revolutions across Europe, when the Prussian army killed over 250 people during uprisings in Berlin. In 1861, King Wilhelm I came to the throne, and the Rotes Rathaus (Red Town Hall) was built to provide a headquarters for the city council. Wilhelm appointed Otto von Bismarck as his prime minister; over the next nine years, Bismarck masterminded the unification of the various German states. After several wars and the defeat of France in 1871, King Wilhelm I became the first German emperor (Kaiser) crowned at Versailles in Paris. Berlin became the capital of the German Empire.

Imperial Capital

After its defeat in the Franco-Prussian War (1870–1871), France was obliged to pay a huge amount of money (war reparations) to the new German Empire. This money helped fund the next period of expansion in Berlin. Known as *Gründerzeit* (Foundation Years), this economic boom attracted thousands more to the city. Berlin's

"Berlin is . . . frequently called die Kaiserstadt, *the Emperor's city."*

—Jules Laforgue, French poet, writing in the 1880s.

population expanded rapidly; the city's one million inhabitants in 1877 doubled to two million by 1905 and doubled again by 1914. Many of these workers ended up in slumlike tenements known as *Mietskasernen* (rental barracks). Political organizations such as the Social Democratic Party (SPD), founded in 1875, were formed to work against such conditions.

The years before World War I were a flourishing time in the intellectual and cultural life of Berlin, with a new opera house and many new art galleries. Berlin became a center for an artistic movement known as the Berliner Secession led by Max Liebermann and Walter Leistikow. World-renowned scientists worked in the city as well, including physicists Albert Einstein and Max Planck. The political situation was not so promising, however, as, led by Kaiser Wilhelm II, Germany moved toward war.

World War I and After

World War I started in 1914. At first, the war had little impact in Berlin. By 1917, however, food shortages in the capital provoked riots and increasing antiwar activity. The end of the war and Germany's defeat in November 1918 forced Kaiser Wilhelm II to give up the throne, marking the end of more than five hundred years of

◀ *Karl Liebknecht, one of the leaders of the communist Spartacus League, is shown here addressing a crowd on January 4, 1919. Less than two weeks later, members of the Freikorps (World War I veterans) brutally murdered Liebknecht and his coleader, Rosa Luxemburg.*

Hohenzollern rule. In Berlin, the SPD declared Germany to be a Democratic Republic, while members of the communist Spartacus League declared the Free Socialist Republic of Germany. In 1919, Freikorps troops (soldiers who had returned from the war) ruthlessly put down an uprising of Spartacus League supporters. As the SPD took control, leaders of the Spartacus League were murdered and their bodies dumped in the Landwehr Canal in Berlin. Soon after, the SPD gained the majority of votes in national elections. Berlin was considered too dangerous for the new parliament, however, so the government moved to the small town of Weimar, which gave its name to the first German republic.

The Weimar Republic

In 1920, the city government reorganized and enlarged the area considered Berlin, combining the old city with eight formerly independent suburban towns. The creation of Gross-Berlin (Greater Berlin) increased the area of the city by thirteen times its original size; it now included nearly four million inhabitants. Rising unemployment, strikes, and frequent food shortages, plagued the city. There was great political instability, including assassinations and attempts to unseat the government. Berlin, however, flourished once again as a vibrant cultural center, although with a reputation for personal indulgence and moral and artistic decay. People flocked to Berlin's cabarets, theaters, concert halls, and art galleries to experience the work of artists such as the playwright Bertolt Brecht, composer Kurt Weill, and the artist George Grosz.

The Great Depression of the 1930s, when countries all over the world experienced economic difficulties, brought an end to the fragile Weimar Republic. By the beginning of 1930, almost a quarter of all Berliners were out of work, and riots spread throughout the city. Such instability paved the way for the rise of the extremist National Socialist German Workers' Party (the Nazi Party). In 1933, Nazi Adolf Hitler was appointed German chancellor. In the same year, a fire in the Reichstag, the

Olympic Games

In 1936, the Olympic Games were held in Berlin. A huge Olympic stadium was built for the Games, the western part of the city was cleaned up, trees were planted, and new subways and train lines were constructed. The Nazis did not want the world to witness the worse excesses of their rule, however, so notices banning Jews from entering public buildings were removed, and Nazi supporters were ordered not to bully and attack Jews for the duration of the Games. There was international outrage, however, when the Nazis banned Jews from the German Olympic teams, and they were forced to withdraw the ban. Although the Games fooled many foreigners into believing that all was well in Nazi Germany, the Nazis did not have it all their own way. The African American athlete Jesse Owens won four gold medals, a fact that did not sit comfortably with Nazi theories of the supremacy of the blond-haired, blue-eyed Aryan race.

Parliament building, gave the Nazis an excuse to arrest their political opponents. Soon after, opposition parties such as the SPD were banned, and Hitler's Nazi Party, the democratically elected majority in parliament, ruled alone. Hitler soon ruled as a dictator with his government based in Berlin, once again the capital of Germany.

Kristallnacht

Jews quickly became a prime target for the Nazis. Jewish businesses were boycotted, Jews were prohibited from doing many jobs, and, in 1935, all non-Aryans lost their German citizenship. Many Jews fled abroad. Others were forced to crowd into walled ghettoes and to wear a Star of David on

▲ *During the Allies' capture of Berlin in 1945, the Reichstag stood in ruins, as pictured here with Soviet warplanes flying overhead.*

their clothes to identify themselves as Jews. In 1938, violence increased as Jewish shops, businesses, synagogues, and houses in Berlin and all over Germany were attacked and looted on the night of November 9 through 10, known as Kristallnacht, "Night of Broken Glass." Thousands of Jews were rounded up and taken to concentration camps. By the end of World War II in 1945, an estimated twelve million civilians across Europe, including at least six million Jews, had been murdered, all by Hitler's orders.

World War II

Hitler took Germany to war in 1939, starting World War II. Most people in Berlin still remembered the severe difficulties—the lack of food, the loss of money's buying power, and the electricity and gas shortages—of World War I and after and did not support Hitler's actions. By this time, however, Hitler had gained complete control over the army and savagely attacked his German opponents.

The first Allied bombs dropped on the city in 1940, and much of the city was reduced to rubble during the Battle of Berlin from 1943 to 1944. Tens of thousands of civilians were killed and thousands more made homeless. The war came to an end in 1945 with the final battle for Berlin, as Hitler committed suicide in his bunker.

Trümmerfrauen

By the end of the war, Berlin was in ruins. Entire neighborhoods were nothing but rubble; there was no gas, electricity, water, or public transportation. Clearing the rubble took years and was largely carried out by women, known as *Trümmerfrauen* (rubble women). They created huge hills of junk that still exist today.

Under the Yalta Agreement between the Allies, Berlin was divided into four zones, with the Soviets controlling eight districts in the east and the British, French, and Americans maintaining twelve districts in the west. As repayment for their costs in fighting World War II, the Soviets took apart factories and transported the equipment back to the Union of Soviet Socialist Republics (also known as the USSR or Soviet Union). They also forcibly rounded up thousands of men in Berlin and moved them to labor camps in the Soviet Union.

The Berlin Airlift

Relations between the former Allies soon began to break down over Berlin. In 1948, the British, French, and Americans decided to merge their zones to create West Berlin. The Soviets, whose land completely surrounded West Berlin, responded by blockading West Berlin with troops to prevent any supplies entering the city. For nearly a year, British and American planes

"The rare case where the conquered is very satisfied with the conqueror."

—Konrad Adenauer, Chancellor of Germany, on the Allied occupation of West Germany, 1960.

Berlin Wall

The construction of the Berlin Wall took Berliners by surprise. The operation started on August 13, 1961, when East German troops blocked off all the roads, subways, and train lines running between East and West Berlin. They quickly erected a barbed wire fence that split the city in two. The first concrete block was put into place on August 15. The windows and doors of houses along or across the border were bricked up, although at first many people escaped by jumping from upper-floor windows onto outstretched sheets held by rescuers on the Western side. By the 1970s, however, the wall was a giant concrete structure, about 28 miles (42 km) long, which zigzagged through the city, with electric fences, trenches, and dogs on the eastern side. Other walls and barriers were also built around the rest of West Berlin to seal it off from the surrounding East German countryside.

delivered all supplies into West Berlin by air, a process known as the Berlin Airlift. The Soviets finally backed down in 1949 and allowed supplies into the city.

Berlin remained split into two parts—West and East. Germany itself was divided into the Federal Republic of Germany (West Germany), with its capital at Bonn, and the German Democratic Republic (GDR or East Germany), with its capital at East Berlin.

Geographically, the Soviet-controlled GDR surrounded West Berlin. Opponents of

▲ *In November 1989, cranes began removing sections of the Berlin Wall while crowds of Berliners looked on.*

the communist system of the Soviet Union saw West Berlin as a showpiece for capitalism, and millions of dollars flowed in to rebuild it. At first, people were permitted to move between the GDR and West Germany; the transportation system in Berlin still covered the whole city. Then, in 1952, the GDR sealed its border with West Germany.

As conditions worsened for people in the GDR, a flood of emigrants from east to west was channeled through West Berlin. Thousands of people left the GDR by this route, causing a crisis in the East German economy. To stop this outflow, the Soviet authorities began constructing the Berlin Wall on August 13, 1961. The wall physically divided the city into East and West Berlin and prevented people from moving between the two parts.

Division and Reunification

The wall divided Berlin for twenty-eight years. During that time, West Berlin was kept going by massive amounts of money from West Germany, although its population declined. Change came in 1989 when Hungary opened its western border, creating a legal route for East Germans who wanted to move to the West. Thousands of people left East Germany, and thousands more demonstrated for reform at home. The demonstrators' slogan was "We are one people." On November 9, 1989, the East German government granted free movement to its citizens; people began to flock across the wall, which was destroyed by East German border guards and demolition crews in the weeks that followed.

In 1990, Germany became a unified country once again. Berlin regained its position as the capital of Germany in 1991, and the government moved into the restored Reichstag building in 1999.

CHAPTER 2

People of Berlin

Since reunification in 1990, the population of Berlin has fallen slightly to its present level of around 3.4 million inhabitants. Many people have moved out of the city to live in the surrounding countryside areas in Brandenburg, which was not an option for the population of West Berlin when the wall divided the city.

Of course, Germans make up the largest part of the population. Of the total population in Berlin, people of German descent number roughly 3 million. The ancestry of the German people can be traced back to the various ancient tribes that lived in the area that today forms modern Germany, including the Goths, the Franks, the Saxons, and the Teutons.

A Home for Immigrants

The city has continued its long tradition of attracting immigrants. The legacy of the French Huguenots who came to Berlin in the seventeenth century can still be seen today in Berlin, with delicacies such as the Berlin meatball called by its French name, the *Boulette*. Today, Berlin is the most multicultural place in Germany, with immigrants from about 190 different nations around the world living in the city.

◄ *Every spring, the Karneval der Kulturen takes place in the streets of Kreuzberg. The carnival is a vibrant celebration of multicultural Berlin.*

▶ *Foreigners make up about thirteen percent of Berlin's population. This chart gives a breakdown of the foreign population by countries of origin.*

The largest ethnic group in Berlin is Turkish. These immigrants originally came to West Germany as *Gastarbeiter* (guest workers) from Turkey during the 1950s and 1960s, because the country could not provide enough German workers to support their booming economy. Most Gastarbeiter believed that they would return home after a few years of working in Germany, and at first, there was little attempt to integrate the Turkish immigrants into the German way of life. Many stayed in Germany, however, and today there is a community of about 150,000 Turks in Berlin. The main concentrations of Turkish inhabitants are in western districts of the city, particularly in Kreuzberg, where Turkish shops and businesses line the streets.

Other districts of Berlin that are home to a high proportion of immigrant residents include Tiergarten, Neukölln, and Wedding. Since reunification, many immigrants have come from Poland and countries that were former Soviet republics. Often, they are *Aussiedler*—people of German origin who had settled in the Soviet Union and are now returning to their homeland, including many Jewish families from Russia and the Ukraine. Other large immigrant groups include about 72,000 refugees from the former Yugoslavia, as well as immigrants from Italy and Greece.

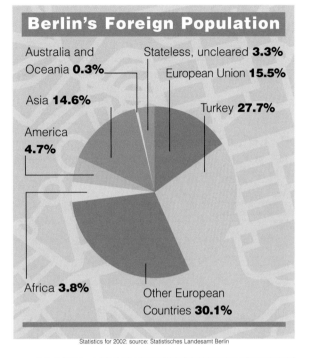

Berlin's Foreign Population

Australia and Oceania **0.3%**

Stateless, uncleared **3.3%**

European Union **15.5%**

Asia **14.6%**

Turkey **27.7%**

America **4.7%**

Africa **3.8%**

Other European Countries **30.1%**

Statistics for 2002: source: Statistisches Landesamt Berlin

Berlin Jews

Officially, Berlin's Jewish population stands at about 12,000. This number is based on only those Jews who are registered at a synagogue; however, the actual number of Berlin Jews is estimated at around 20,000 people. When Hitler came to power in 1933, about 160,000 German Jews lived in Berlin. Within six years, about half of this population had emigrated, been driven out by Nazi anti-Semitic policies, or had been arrested. The Nazis deported about 10,000 Berlin Jews to ghettos in Eastern Europe and 50,000 to their deaths in the concentration camps. About 1,300 Jews managed to survive the war in Berlin, many because they were married to non-Jews or were able to hide. Today, Berlin's Jewish community is thriving again, and there is a wide interest in Jewish culture and cuisine in the city.

▲ *The Neue Synagogue first opened in Berlin in 1866. It suffered severe damage during World War II but was reconstructed and opened again in 1995.*

Religion

Berlin's multicultural population ensures that a wide range of religions are practiced in the city. Only about half of the population of Berlin, however, is a member of a religious community. About one-third of these are Christians.

Berlin has been mainly a Protestant city since the Reformation, particularly after the influx of Protestant Huguenots from France during the seventeenth century. In 2001, almost 24 percent of Berlin's religious community belonged to the Protestant Church and 9 percent to the Roman Catholic Church. Christian services are performed in a wide variety of languages at churches around the city, including Armenian, Bulgarian, Egyptian, Ethiopian, Greek, Korean, and various African languages. The main Christian churches are the Berliner Dom (the cathedral) on Museum Island, the Marienkirche in Mitte for Protestant services, and the Roman Catholic St. Hedwigs-Kathedrale. The Huguenot community has its own church in Gendarmenmarkt, and there are many other churches for different Christian denominations.

Muslims, Jews, and Others

There is a large Muslim community in Berlin, numbering about 206,000 people—6 percent of the city's population. Many of these Muslims come from the Turkish community. Over seventy mosques serve

Muslims in Berlin, and more are planned for construction. The biggest mosque to be completed so far is the Sehitlik Mosque in Neukölln, which can hold up to two thousand worshippers. Its design is based on that of mosques built in Ottoman Turkey in the eighteenth century. It has a huge dome, and its towers, called minarets, rise 122 feet (37 meters). Many mosques, however, are in converted buildings such as warehouses.

Before Kristallnacht, the largest of the eighty synagogues in Berlin was the Neue Synagogue in Oranienburger Strasse, in the heart of Scheunenviertel, the old Jewish quarter of Berlin. It was partly destroyed by the Nazis and then further damaged by Allied bombs. Today, its huge golden dome and magnificent façade have been restored, and it houses a Jewish center and prayer hall.

The Nazis destroyed many of Berlin's synagogues during Kristallnacht. Three synagogues, however, did survive and are used for worship by the city's Jewish population today. The synagogue on Rykestrasse, northeast of Mitte, is the biggest synagogue in Germany. It survived Kristallnacht because of its location—tucked away in a courtyard and surrounded by houses. During the war, it was used as a munitions store, but it was restored in the 1950s and was the only place of worship for the small Jewish community who lived in East Berlin. The Nazis set fire to the synagogue on Pestalozzistrasse in western Berlin, but it presented such a hazard to the surrounding houses that the Berlin fire department put out the blaze. Today, it is one of the most popular places in the city for Jewish worship. Only a side wing survives of the third synagogue, the once magnificent Fraenkelufer Synagogue in Kreuzberg.

The city also has members of many other religious groups, such as Hindus and Buddhists. There are many centers in Berlin where people can learn more about the beliefs and practices of Buddhism.

Seasonal Markets

Christmas and Easter are both celebrated in the city with large seasonal markets. At Christmas, Yuletide markets are found all over the city, such as the one at Gendarmenmarkt (pictured left). These markets sell traditional toys, hotspiced wine, and delicious ginger cookies. The Easter markets are found around Alexanderplatz in Mitte and Kaiser-Wilhelm-Gedächtniskirche in western Berlin.

◀ *Lively cafes and restaurants that line a series of connected courtyards make Hakesche Höfe a popular meeting place. Recently renovated, these buildings were constructed in the early twentieth century in the Secessionist style.*

From Pastries to Pork

Berliners have a wide choice of places to buy food, ranging from the cheapest supermarkets to specialty stores selling high-quality produce. Most Berliners shop for specific food items at local markets, butchers' shops, bakeries, fruit and vegetable stores, and health-food stores. Pastry shops and bakeries are very popular for items such as the *Berliner*, a type of doughnut, or fresh *Schrippen*, the Berlin word for *Brötchen*, or bread rolls. Supermarkets such as Aldi, Netto, and Plus offer the most basic products at the lowest prices, while Reichelt, Meyer, Ullrich, and Kaiser's are fancier and more expensive stores. For real treats, wealthy Berliners go to the luxury food halls in Galeries Lafayette and KaDeWe (short for Kaufhaus des Westens,

"Department Store of the West"). A French store, Galeries Lafayette, stocks French specialties such as cheese. The food hall on the sixth floor of KaDeWe is a legend throughout Berlin, with its sumptuous displays of luxurious food.

Traditional local cooking centers on pork with cabbage and potatoes—the only crops that grew successfully in the light soil of the region. An example of a traditional dish is *Eisbein*, made from pig's feet. Other local dishes often eaten in Berlin homes include liver with onions and apples and *Kasseler Rippen*, which are smoked pork chops. Beer is the most popular alcoholic beverage, and the city has several local breweries including Berliner Kindl and Engelhardt. Although wine is not produced locally, German wines from the Rhine and Mosel regions are always popular.

Berliners love to eat out, and they have a huge range of options to choose from. One of the favorite fast foods in the city is the *Currywurst*. This spicy sausage in a bread roll is smothered with warm ketchup and curry powder. Another very popular snack is the *doner kebab*, spiced meat, which is usually a mixture of veal and lamb, sliced thinly and stuffed inside a pita bread with salad and a yogurt dressing. Coffeehouses

▲ The sumptuous food hall at KaDeWe (Kaufhaus des Westens, Department Store of the West) offers Berliners the chance to buy a huge variety of exotic, expensive, luxurious foods from around the world.

and cafes are very popular in the city, and Berliners visit these places at any time of the day for a light meal or simply for a drink. Stopping for *Kaffee und Kuchen,* "coffee and cakes," is a popular way to while away an afternoon. Restaurants are often packed on weekends, and the choice of cuisine is huge, ranging from Italian to Thai and Turkish to Vietnamese.

Berlin Breakfasts

Breakfast is an important meal in Berlin. Berliners invite friends for breakfast, and on weekends many people go out for long breakfasts that merge into lunch (to become brunch). Berlin breakfasts are not simply cereal and toast. Breakfast menus often include a range of cold meats and cheeses, yogurt, fruit, scrambled eggs, smoked salmon, bread, butter, and jam. On Sundays, many cafes serve brunches throughout the morning that include hot dishes such as pasta, quiche, meat, or vegetable casseroles.

CHAPTER 3

Living in Berlin

Berlin today is the product of its unique history as a divided city. Since the wall came down in 1989, efforts have concentrated on knitting together the city once again, and architecture has played a large part in this process.

Housing

After the devastation of World War II, housing became a priority for the governments in both East and West Berlin. In East Berlin, projects such as the Stalinallee, built from 1951 to 1954 and now renamed Karl-Marx-Allee, helped meet this need. The buildings of Stalinallee were constructed in a style that was approved by the communist government of the Soviet Union. They housed *Volkspalaste* (people's palaces), small apartments for workers. A huge boulevard 295-feet (90-meters) wide was lined with these massive structures, which rose seven to nine stories high. Today, they have been preserved, and their crumbling fronts are being restored.

In West Berlin, the government responded to the housing problem with projects such as the experimental Hansaviertel estate. In both West and East

◄ *The huge buildings that line the Karl-Marx-Allee were built in the 1950s. The Soviet architects who designed the buildings were obliged to use the "wedding-cake style" approved by the Communist Party.*

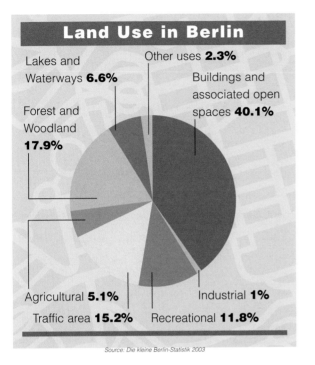

Land Use in Berlin

- Lakes and Waterways **6.6%**
- Other uses **2.3%**
- Buildings and associated open spaces **40.1%**
- Forest and Woodland **17.9%**
- Agricultural **5.1%**
- Traffic area **15.2%**
- Recreational **11.8%**
- Industrial **1%**

Source: Die kleine Berlin-Statistik 2003

Hansaviertel

The Hansaviertel estate lies on the northwest side of the Tiergarten in northwest Berlin. It was built between 1953 and 1957 on a World War II bomb site in time for the International Architectural Exhibition in 1957, which had as its theme the "city of tomorrow." Fifty well-known architects from thirteen different countries, including Walter Gropius and the Finnish architect Alvar Aalto, designed the buildings to make up a varied community in a green setting. Today, Hansaviertel is home to about thirty-five hundred people and has its own shops, churches, library, and school.

Berlin, prefabricated buildings—buildings made in sections ready for assembly on site—were put up with great speed. The German-born architect Walter Gropius designed the glass and concrete high-rise buildings that make up Gropiusstadt in southwest Berlin. About fifty thousand people live in these apartments. In East Berlin, prefabricated housing developments were constructed at Marzahn, Hellersdorf, and Hohenschönhausen. These contained row after row of high-rise buildings containing tiny, identical apartments. Because they had indoor bathrooms, heating, and parking, the apartments were still more attractive than much of the older housing. Today, these inner-city areas are being renovated and improved and are attracting new tenants.

Building Projects

The huge challenge faced by Berliners after the wall came down was to unify their city once again. Some building projects have provided a focus for this process, the most famous being the renovation of the parliament building, located in the former West Berlin, to house the German government. British architect Sir Norman Foster designed a huge glass dome to sit in the center of the old building with a cone of

"...Berlin is a very young city, for music, for theater, for science, and for universities..."

—Berlin Mayor Klaus Wowereit, 2003.

25

mirrors at its center that reflect light into the parliamentary building below. Another huge project, Potsdamer Platz provides Berlin with a new financial and business center and includes buildings designed by a range of top international architects.

▼ *French architect Jean Nouvel designed the ultramodern building that houses the department store Galeries Lafayette. The store sells French goods ranging from food to clothes.*

Stores and Markets

Berlin has a wide range of different types of stores and markets. Since the reunification of the city, the Potsdamer Platz has been redeveloped with the intention of providing a central focal point for Berlin. Because of Berlin's time as a divided city, however, each neighborhood has its own shopping center, and many Berliners continue to do much of their shopping in their local area rather than heading for the city center. The main areas for shopping include Kurfurstendamm,

Searching for Bargains

▶ *Berlin has a long tradition of flea markets, (pictured right) where people go to browse and find bargains among stalls selling books, furniture, jewelry, paintings, and second-hand clothes. Some of the most popular weekend flea markets include the Kunst und Nostalgiemarkt in Mitte and the Flohmarkt Spandau. Other markets sell fresh food—for example, the market at the Winterfeldtplatz in Schöneberg, the Turkish Market in Kreuzberg, and the farmers' market at Wittenbergplatz. Three indoor market halls survive from the late nineteenth century, built to move street markets indoors. Today, these ornate structures house food stalls as well as stalls selling toys and other items.*

Friedrichstrasse, Wedding, Friedrichshain, Schöneberg, and Tiergarten. There are many large shopping malls, but there is still a strong tradition of alternative, small shops selling items such as bric-a-brac, second-hand clothes, books, and art.

Berliners tend to buy quality goods in specialty stores or markets and use supermarkets for everyday groceries and other basic items. Since the 1990s, there has been a marked increase in the number of large shopping malls; Berlin now has more than thirty-five. As well as places to shop, many have become social centers, with attractions such as movie theaters, bowling alleys, and fitness facilities. Some people think that they take customers away from neighborhood stores, however. One of the most popular of these shopping centers is the Potsdamer Platz Arkaden, which attracts tens of thousands of visitors every day. Most stores open from ten to eight every day except Sunday, when they shut at four. Twice a year, in January and July, stores in Berlin have big sales.

Berlin's vibrant cultural life has encouraged a booming trade in art, books, and antiques. There are many long-established art galleries in Charlottenburg, while the newer galleries in Mitte tend to show and sell more experimental, contemporary art. Antique shops are found throughout Berlin, and many Berliners love to spend their spare time looking in these shops and at the flea markets.

Education

Germany's early-education system is run independently by the sixteen states that make up the country, while the federal government is responsible for students' education once they complete their compulsory schooling at age sixteen or older. Berlin has broadly the same system as the other German states with children required to go to school for ten years. Children may attend free public schools financed by the state, or their parents may pay for them to go to private schools.

Children usually start compulsory school at the age of six, although many attend kindergarten for two or three years before this. They attend *Grundschule* (elementary school) for six years. As well as public primary schools, there are twenty-four private elementary schools in Berlin, including Protestant and Catholic schools, a Jewish school, and an Islamic school.

After elementary school, children and their parents have to decide among several options. *Hauptschule* is a vocational school—

Universities

Berlin is Germany's largest university center with four universities: the Freie Universität (Free University), the Technische Universität (Technical University), the Humboldt Universität, and the Universität der Künste (University of the Arts). When the city was split after World War II, the Humboldt University was in the Soviet zone. The Free University was established in 1948 to provide higher education for students in the western zone. Berlin also has several arts and technical colleges.

one that trains students for a particular job, trade, or profession—and pupils study there for three years. *Realschule's* classes teach technical skills and those used in businesses; pupils attend for four years. *Gymnasium* emphasizes academics, and pupils spend seven years studying before taking the Abitur, an exam that must be passed to enter a university. There is also *Gesamtschule* (comprehensive school), which is a combination of the other three forms of high school. Children who take up *Hauptschule* and *Realschule* usually go on to some kind of apprentice-training program combining both study and work.

Berlin has many specialist high schools, which students start at age twelve. The Coubertin grammar school, the Flatow senior school, and the Werner Seelenbinder school are all boarding schools that emphasize athletic training. A school farm stands on the island of Scharfenberg in the

▲ *Children at a primary school in Berlin take part in a biology lesson. The girl in the foreground is wearing a traditional Muslim headscarf.*

borough of Reinickendorf. The State Ballet School prepares students for an apprenticeship as stage dancers. Berlin's ten private high schools include the Catholic Canisius-Kolleg and the Protestant Gymnasium Zum Grauen Kloster. There are also several international schools in Berlin, including the John F. Kennedy School, the French Grammar School, the British School, the Swedish School, and the Japanese School.

Some schools in Berlin offer bilingual teaching. It is estimated that up to 20 percent of Berlin's schoolchildren speak German as a second language, and half of this number speak Turkish. Since 1992, there have been "European" schools in Berlin, where equal numbers of German and non-German speakers are taught in German and another language. The aim of these schools is to ensure that students become fluent in both languages. European schools in Berlin offer many languages, including French, English, Russian, Polish, Spanish, or Turkish.

Planes and Trains

Berlin has two main airports; Berlin Tegel is 5 miles (8 km) northwest of the city's center, while Berlin Schönefeld is 11 miles (18 km) southeast. A third airport stands in the city's center, Berlin Tempelhof, which handles domestic and private flights. Berlin Tegel is the busiest of the three airports, but this situation will change soon because Schönefeld is due for a huge expansion.

Germany has an excellent train system, and Berlin is linked with many European cities by direct trains. The main station for international train travel is Bahnhof Zoo, although a new international station is under construction. There are also links by express coaches on the autobahns, or expressways.

Getting around Berlin

As a divided city, Berlin had two separate transportation systems. Today, the two systems have largely been knit together again to provide an excellent public transportation system. The Berlin public transportation company (BVG) and the railway company Deutsche Bahn AG together run Berlin's public transportation system. The suburban railway (S-Bahn) network is about 200 miles (320 km) long, and during 2002, 305 million passengers traveled on the fifteen S-Bahn lines. The underground railway (U-Bahn) has ten lines.

There are also local buses and, in the eastern part of the city, streetcars. The city is divided into three zones for pricing, and the same ticket can be used on the S-Bahn, U-Bahn, local buses, and streetcars. The city of Berlin also has an agreement with the surrounding federal state of Brandenburg to coordinate timetables between the different transportation companies and to use uniform ticket and pricing systems.

Cyclists can enjoy many bicycle lanes in Berlin, particularly in the western part of the city. Although there are problems with traffic jams, driving in Berlin is usually easier than in most European capitals because the city was rebuilt after World War II with a modern layout. Especially in the eastern part of city, however, reconstruction work can still cause problems for motorists.

Environmental Issues

Berlin suffers from the effects of pollution, particularly air pollution and acid rain, which has affected many of the trees in the city. To address the damage caused by burning fossil fuels such as gas and diesel, the government is encouraging the use of natural gas as a fuel for vehicles. There is also a move to use solar energy to provide the electrical power needed in new buildings. Berlin's lakes, rivers, and canals are badly polluted, and efforts are being made to clean them up. Berlin, however, is the only large city in Germany that obtains all its drinking water from its own supplies of groundwater without the need to import water from elsewhere.

Pig Problems

Berlin has an unusual problem for a capital city—wild pigs. It is estimated that there are around twenty thousand pigs living wild in and around the city, many in the huge Grunewald forest in the west of the city.

Travel by Boat

The waterway network in Berlin includes the Spree (pictured above) *and Havel Rivers and a large number of canals. There are fifteen public ports; Westhafen is the largest. The water network is used to carry cargo, and in 2002, about 3.4 million tons (3.1 million metric tons) of cargo were transported by this route. The waterways offer opportunities for recreation and tourism; many companies offer pleasure trips through the city and farther afield to destinations such as the lakes of Müggelsee in the southeast of the city.*

Their population has grown rapidly due to mild winters and an abundance of food available in the city. The pigs cause damage to gardens and parks, raid garbage cans, and are a menace on Berlin's roads, where they are a danger to traffic. Wild pigs even dug up the Hertha soccer club's field. The Berlin government employs licensed hunters to try to keep the pig population under control, and from 2002 to 2003, over two thousand pigs were killed. Another solution is to feed a pill to the pigs that will make them temporarily unable to have piglets.

CHAPTER 4

Berlin at Work

Since 1920, Berlin has been a separate federal state, making it one of the three (with Hamburg and Bremen) city-states of the sixteen federal states that make up modern Germany. Berlin's House of Representatives (*Abgeordnetenhaus*) meets in the restored building of the former Prussian state parliament. The House of Representatives is made up of at least 130 representatives elected by the people of Berlin for four-year terms. The main purpose of the House of Representatives is to debate, change, and pass legislation and to supervise the Senate.

The House of Representatives elects a mayor, and he or she then suggests eight senators who are elected individually. The senators form the Senate, and each of them has responsibility for a different department: justice; finance; economics and technology; urban development; education, youth, and sports; labor, social affairs, and women's issues; and science, research, and culture. This central administration decides on the planning and control of the development of the city as a whole. Public authorities such as the police and the fire

◀ *A symbol of the importance of "openness" in German democracy, a spectacular glass dome topping the restored Reichstag building allows members of the public to see straight down into the parliament hall.*

department are also directly under the control of the central administration. The Rotes Rathaus (Red Town Hall) is the seat of the mayor of Berlin and the Senate.

The main parties in Berlin's political life are the Christian Democrats (CDU), the Social Democratic Party (SPD), the Free Democratic Party (FDP), the Party of Democratic Socialism (PDS), and the Green Party. In 2001, Klaus Wowereit of the SDP was elected mayor of Berlin.

National Government

The federal state of Berlin sends representatives to the German Federal Council, and Berlin's voters also elect members of the German parliament, the Bundestag. Since 1999, Berlin has been the seat of national government in Germany. The move from Bonn to Berlin brought an estimated fifteen thousand extra people to live and work in Berlin. A government district has been established around the restored Reichstag, including new embassies and a new Federal Chancellery building.

Berlin's Economy

Germany has one of the world's largest economies, but it has suffered some setbacks in recent years, and the economy of Berlin

"Berlin is a German Land and at the same time a City."

—Constitution of Berlin, September 1, 1950.

reflects this. Berlin also has its own peculiar problems as a result of its recent history. At the time of reunification, East Berlin had some manufacturing industries but most of them used out-of-date machinery and methods, and many were closed down in the early 1990s. West Berlin had little industry or manufacturing because it had been effectively isolated during the years of the Cold War. Both halves of the city had relied on massive subsidies to prop up their economies, which came to an end once the city was reunited.

Problems after Reunification

At first, reunification helped the economy grow, but very soon the city faced problems. One result of being divided into two separate parts was that the city did not have a well-developed infrastructure for business; vital links such as transportation and communications needed massive reorganization after reunification. The huge building projects that were undertaken all over Berlin during the 1990s pushed the city near to bankruptcy. In 2001, Berlin's longstanding Christian Democrat mayor, Eberhard Diepgen, was voted out as a result of the financial problems caused by excessive spending and corruption.

Signs of Recovery

The city still has a huge debt, but there are some hopeful signs that its economy is beginning to recover. The state and national government employ large numbers of people in Berlin. Some major multinational companies such as Sony have moved into Berlin, particularly into the new business and financial center at Potsdamer Platz. It is mainly small- and medium-sized companies, however, that are driving Berlin's recovery, and most of these are in the service sector— for example, banking, commerce, the hotel and restaurant business, construction, and tourism. Berlin's remaining manufacturing industries have been updated over recent years, including electrical engineering, vehicle manufacturing, chemical and medicine production, and mechanical engineering.

Berlin has many attractions for businesses. After reunification, all the telecommunications systems had to be completely replaced. As a result, Berlin today has an excellent communications infrastructure with more than 105,000 miles (170,000 km) of fiber-optic cable and a digitized telephone network. Berlin's location bridges Eastern and Western Europe and offers businesses good education and science facilities and an excellent supply of qualified workers.

The city government has set up several projects to link businesses and the research departments of its universities. One example is the MediaCity Adlershof, a technology park combining university departments and high-tech industries. Areas of future expansion include the media, transportation technology, information and communications technology, and environmental technology. Financial services have also become increasingly important, although Frankfurt is still Germany's leading financial center. In particular, the Berlin stock exchange has built a reputation for trading with Eastern European companies.

Tourism

Tourism has increased in importance since the wall came down in 1989. Millions of people visit Berlin each year to experience the unique history and atmosphere of the German capital. More than 4.75 million people stayed in Berlin hotel rooms in 2002, and many new hotels are opening their doors for business. One example is the luxury Ritz-Carlton Hotel in Potsdamer Platz, which opened in January 2004.

Berlin's Problems

One of the main priorities for the federal government of Berlin is to reduce the city's massive debts. Berlin needs to cut about 10 percent of the city's budget to bring the debt under control; the government plans to reduce spending on investment and to cut some jobs. As part of this cost-cutting campaign, some public facilities such as swimming pools and three theaters have been closed down. Berlin still has a high unemployment rate—around 18 percent in 2003—and reducing this rate, especially among young and immigrant workers, is a major challenge.

▲ *Many Berliners take part in anti-Nazi rallies against the extremist right-wing National Democratic Party (NPD). The picture shows a rally held in 2000 with people carrying banners in German and English.*

Ossis and Wessis

Some problems are a direct result of Berlin's history as a divided city. At the time of reunification, people who lived in West Berlin generally had a much higher standard of living than those in the former East Berlin. The gap between the levels of pay and standards of living was the cause of some friction between *Ossis* (Easterners) and *Wessis* (Westerners). This gap has since been narrowed, but discontent among some Ossis has been reflected in the growing popularity of the Party of Democratic Socialism (PDS), which grew out of the East German Communist Party that once dominated East Berlin. The PDS won a lot of votes in the areas of the former East Berlin in the elections of 2001.

Demonstrations held in Berlin in 2000 and 2001 underline another problem area in Berlin and in Germany as a whole; support is growing for the neo-Nazi National Democratic Party (NPD), which wants to end immigration into Germany. Berliners are protesting this trend, however; huge antiracist demonstrations in Berlin and other German cities matched demonstrations held by the NDP.

"Right-wing extremism is the greatest threat there is at the moment for German democracy"

—Heinz Fromm, Office for the Protection of the Constitution, 2001.

CHAPTER 5

Berlin at Play

Berlin is the cultural center of Germany, an exciting and vibrant place for nightlife, drama, art, music, dance, and movies. It also has a wide range of cultural festivals throughout the year. To find out what is happening in their city, Berliners consult the magazines *Zitty* and *Tip*.

Performing Arts

The city features one of the world's most famous classical orchestras, the Berlin Philharmonic. The orchestra's home is the Philharmonie, completed in 1963 according to German architect Hans Scharoun's unusual design, which places the orchestra in the center of the auditorium with the seats all around. Berlin also supports six other classical orchestras, as well as three opera houses including the Deutsche Oper Berlin and the Staatsoper.

Every other kind of musical taste is catered for in Berlin, from jazz to big rock bands to world music. The main venues for large pop concerts are the Olympia Stadion, the stadium built by the Nazis to host the 1936 Olympic Games; the Velodrom; the Max-Schmeling-Hall, which is home to Berlin's baseball team; and the Waldbühne,

◄ *Berlin's Love Parade takes place on the second Saturday of July, a celebration of techno music and dance. Here, revelers crowd around the Siegessäule, the triumphal column in the center of the Tiergarten.*

an amphitheater that can hold up to twenty thousand people. A popular venue for world music is the Haus der Kulturen der Welt (House of World Culture) in the Tiergarten.

Berlin has long been an important center for theater. At the beginning of the twentieth century, actor-director Max Reinhardt became internationally famous for his work at the Deutsches Theater. The German playwright Bertolt Brecht also wrote plays for the Deutsches Theater and for the Berliner Ensemble, where *The Threepenny Opera* had its first performance in 1928. During the Cold War, theaters were built in both the western and eastern parts of the city, and large amounts of money poured into the arts. After reunification, some theaters were forced to close down, but Berlin still has many major venues including the Deutsches Theater, the Volksbühne, the Schaubühne, and the Hebbel-Theater. Berlin also has a long tradition of performances of cabaret, and a new theater for musicals, the Musical Theater Berlin, opened in 1999 at the Potsdamer Platz.

All kinds of dance, from classical to disco to techno, are popular in Berlin. An important part of the cultural scene in Berlin, modern dance can be seen at venues such as the Hebbel-Theater, the Theater am Halleschen Ufer, and the Sophiensaele. Berlin also has three ballet companies. Many performing arts events are held in "cultural centers," often in former warehouses or

Marlene Dietrich

The famous film actress (pictured above) was born in Berlin in 1901. Her real name was Marie Magdalena von Losch. She worked at the Deutsches Theater before starting to get parts in the silent movies being made at the time. She came to the attention of Hollywood when she starred in The Blue Angel, *a "talking" film. She went to the United States, becoming a citizen in 1937, and stayed there throughout World War II, continuing to make movies. Although she lived in Paris at the end of her life, she wanted to be buried in her home city, and her grave lies in the Friedhof III cemetery in western Berlin.*

similar places, with spaces for many different events going on side by side. Berlin is also the European capital for techno music, and every July the city hosts the Love Parade. This event started out as a demonstration for love and peace, but it has become a huge celebration of techno music, when more than one million people pour into the Tiergarten and surrounding area to dance to the music and enjoy themselves.

Cinema

Berlin is the film capital of Germany, with hundreds of theaters ranging from multiplexes to arts cinemas to the huge open-air screenings during summer evenings at the Waldbühne amphitheater. The famous Studio UFA stands just outside Berlin at Bebelsberg, near Potsdam. Established in the early twentieth century, this film studio

▲ *One of the most impressive exhibits in the Pergamon Museum in Berlin is a complete gate from the ancient city of Babylon, dating from the sixth century B.C.*

produced elaborate and classic movies such as *Metropolis*. During the Nazi period, Hitler's propaganda minister Joseph Goebbels used the film studios to produce Nazi propaganda movies. Today, movies are still made at the studios, after a brief closing during the 1990s.

Museums

Museum Island in the Spree River is the site of many of Berlin's most prestigious museums including the Old National Gallery. The Pergamon Museum contains one of the finest collections of archaeological exhibits in the world, with antiquities from ancient Greece and Rome and from the Near East as well as

Haus am Checkpoint Charlie

From 1961 to 1990, Checkpoint Charlie was the main gateway for non-Germans who wanted to pass between West and East Berlin. Today, it is a museum that tells the history of the Berlin Wall and commemorates all those who tried to cross it. Of the 5,000 people who tried to escape from east to west, 191 died in the attempt. One of the most infamous escape attempts occurred in 1962, when a youth called Peter Fechtner was shot by East German guards as he tried to scale the wall. He was then left to bleed to death in the no-man's-land that ran alongside the wall.

countless treasures of Islamic art. The Bode Museum has recently been renovated. It opened in 2005, housing collections of Byzantine art, coins, sculpture, and including a children's gallery.

One of the most famous museums in Berlin opened in 2001—the Jüdisches Museum (Jewish Museum), designed by the Polish architect Daniel Libeskind and one of the most exciting pieces of twentieth-century architecture. The building is in the shape of a long zigzag, partly based on the idea of an opened Star of David. The exhibitions inside commemorate the history of the German Jewish community.

Festivals throughout the Year

Berlin hosts a wide variety of cultural and other festivals throughout the year, ranging from dog shows to jazz festivals to a festival for motorcyclists. The Berliner Festwochen in September includes an array of international events from classical concerts to exhibitions. In the summer, many concerts and other events are held outside, for example, the Classic Open Air festival in Gendarmenmarkt. Every February, Berlin's international film festival attracts stars from all over the world. Other cultural events include the Jazzfest held in November and a theater festival in May. Held for three days in the spring, the Karneval der Kulturen is a celebration of multicultural Berlin. The Oktoberfest is a traditional beer and food festival.

Recreation and Sports

Sports play an important role in many Berliner's lives and are encouraged by the city government as good both for health and for promoting a sense of community. Bicycling is a very popular pastime in Germany; Berlin's ultramodern Velodrom, which opened in 1997, attracts huge crowds for the traditional six-day race every January. The Berlin Marathon, held in September, is the third largest in the world, attracting over thirty thousand runners and roller skaters for its 26-mile (42-km) course. Opportunities for swimming in the city abound, with facilities ranging from indoor pools to artificial and natural beaches alongside Berlin's many lakes.

Soccer, golf, and tennis and other racquet sports are all popular. Berlin's main soccer club, Hertha BSC, plays in the

▲ *Hertha BSC supporters wearing the team colors,*
turn the Olympia Stadion into a sea of blue and white.

German Bundesliga (national league), and their home in the city is the Olympia Stadion. Held every year in May, the German Open Women's Tennis Tournament attracts players from all over the world. Basketball and ice hockey are popular spectator sports. Berliners also love to skate in the cold winter months, when the city maintains outdoor ice rinks at Gendarmenmarkt and Alexanderplatz.

Escaping the Streets

Berlin is a very green city, with nearly one third of its total area covered in parks, forests, lakes, and rivers. Berliners never need to travel far to find an escape from the streets of the city, and many of the most popular spots for a day out are a short ride on the U-Bahn. West of the city, beyond Charlottenburg, lies the Grunewald, a large area of forest and lakes. During summer weekends, the trails through the forest are full of people walking, cycling, running, and horseback riding. The lakes are popular places for swimming and sunbathing, as well as sailing and waterskiing.

To escape the city completely, Berliners head into the Brandenburg region that surrounds Berlin. About 60 miles (100 km) southeast of Berlin lies the Spreewald, an area of rivers, streams, and canals that run through forest and farmland. Berliners can reach this area by train, and many make the

Sachsenhausen

About 22 miles (35 km) northwest of Berlin stands one of the Nazi regime's concentration camps. Called Sachsenhausen, it was built in 1936 and today is a museum and memorial to the thousands of people who died there. The first prisoners at Sachsenhausen were political opponents of the Nazi government, but after Kristallnacht, thousands of Jews were taken to the camp. Soviet soldiers liberated the camp in 1945, but the Soviets soon used it again to house war criminals. Thousands more people died there under the Soviet regime between 1945 and 1950.

journey to go hiking along the trails or punting along the waterways. Another popular day out is to Potsdam, a city to the southwest of Berlin, which can also be reached by train. Full of beautiful buildings, Potsdam is the capital of the state of Brandenburg. Visitors also flock to the spectacular Schloss Sanssouci, which was the summer palace of Frederick the Great. The palace stands in a huge park that contains a number of different gardens.

▼ *For a tranquil day away from the city, people head for the canals and rivers of the Spreewald, southeast of Berlin.*

CHAPTER 6

Looking Forward

Berlin's challenge for the future is to complete the process of reunification, bringing together the people of the former West and East Berlins in a truly united Berlin. Some mistrust remains between the Ossis and Wessis—a "wall in people's heads," as it is often expressed. Just after reunification, many Ossis felt that the political forces of the wealthier and more powerful Wessis were in danger of overwhelming them. A huge statue of the Soviet leader Vladimir Lenin that had stood since 1970 in Leninplatz in the former East Berlin became a symbol of this issue. Local Ossis residents wanted to keep the statue, feeling it was part of their Ossis heritage and felt that they were being pushed around by the authorities. Despite their demonstrations, the government broke up the statue in 1991.

Berlin also needs to work hard to knit together its multicultural population. A step forward for Germany's immigrant communities came in 1999, when a new law was passed to allow any child born in Germany with one parent who had lived in the country for at least eight years to claim automatic German citizenship. Before this

◄ *This aerial view of the Potsdamer Platz in Berlin was taken in September 2003. The redevelopment of this area since unification has turned it into a dynamic center for the new Berlin.*

law, it was very difficult for even children of long-established immigrants to Germany to gain citizenship.

Merging with Brandenburg?

Berlin's position as an independent city-state surrounded by the federal state of Brandenburg is also under question. In a referendum in 1996, a merger between the two states was voted down by the people of Brandenburg, although it was approved by Berliners. Since the two states are increasingly coordinating their efforts to develop the region, the issue is under discussion once again. Berlin believes that there are many good arguments in favor of eventually forming a single state.

Tourism is an expanding industry in Berlin, and good communications are vital for its position as a tourist and a business center. The city government hopes to improve transportation services by expanding the Lehrter Bahnhof (railway station) to make it Berlin's main train station and Europe's largest railway hub. Schönefeld airport is also being expanded to become the major airport of the Berlin-Brandenburg region. This new airport, to be called the Berlin-Brandenburg International (BBI), will eventually take all of the air traffic in the region, and after about 2008 or 2009, both Tegel and Tempelhof airports will be closed. BBI is designed to cope with 20 million passengers a year, and travelers will be able to reach Lehrter Bahnhof in just under thirty minutes.

With its work at reunifying not only the city, but the hearts and minds of its citizens, Berlin remains a city in transition. Its efforts to clean up its land and waters, its encouragement of new businesses, and its unique position between Eastern and Western Europe, however, make Berlin a city well on its way to being a vibrant, major world capital.

Remembering

While Berliners look to the future of their city, they also remember its unique history. Sometimes these memories are painful, as people struggle to understand the injustices committed in the past. The Federal Republic of Germany's main site for commemoration is Berlin's Neue Wache (New Guard House), on Unter den Linden, a graceful nineteenth-century building which is a memorial for the "victims of war and tyranny." At the center of the large internal hall stands a single statue of a mother with her dead son. In the former headquarters of the East German secret police, the Stasi, there is now a museum and memorial center. On the shore of Lake Wannsee in western Berlin stands a reminder of one of the most chilling episodes in German Nazi history—the conference held at the villa, Haus der Wannsee, to decide the future of the Jewish people under Nazi rule. Today, the Haus der Wannsee-Konferenz is a memorial for the Holocaust with a museum recounting the human tragedy that followed that fateful meeting.

Time Line

A.D. 100s Various tribes settle along the banks of the Havel and Spree Rivers.

1237 First written reference to Cölln appears.

1307 Berlin and Cölln form an alliance and become Berlin-Cölln.

1359 Berlin-Cölln becomes part of the Hanseatic League, a trading organization.

1415 Friedrich von Hohenzollern becomes Elector of Brandenburg.

1432 Berlin-Cölln are formally united.

1486 Berlin-Cölln is capital of Brandenburg.

1618–48 Thirty Years War devastates Berlin.

1640–88 Friedrich Wilhelm, the "Great Elector," rules and reconstructs Berlin.

1701 Brandenburg becomes a kingdom; Elector Friedrich III becomes king of Brandenburg-Prussia.

1740–86 King Friedrich II (Frederick the Great) rules.

1756–63 Frederick the Great tries to gain more territory with the Seven Years War.

1806 French troops occupy Berlin.

1871 France is defeated; King Wilhelm I becomes first German emperor, and Berlin becomes capital of the German Empire.

1914–18 World War I is fought. At the end of the war, Kaiser Wilhelm II leaves the throne and Hohenzollern rule ends.

1919 Uprising of the Spartacus League is suppressed; Weimar Republic is established.

1933 Adolf Hitler becomes German chancellor; fire damages the Reichstag.

1936 Olympic Games are held in Berlin.

1938 During Kristallnacht, Jewish homes, businesses, and synagogues are destroyed.

1939 World War II begins.

1940 First Allied bombs fall on Berlin.

1943–44 Allies heavily bomb the city.

1945 World War II ends.

1948–49 Soviets prevent West Berlin from getting food and other necessities; Berlin Airlift begins, bringing supplies to the city.

1952 East Germany seals its border with West Germany.

1961 The Berlin Wall is erected.

1989 Germans tear down the Berlin Wall.

1990 East and West Germany are reunified to form the Federal Republic of Germany.

1991 Berlin becomes the capital of a reunified Germany.

1996 In a referendum, Berliners vote to merge Berlin with Brandenburg, but the people of Brandenburg vote against it.

1999 The German government moves into the Reichstag.

Glossary

Allies in World War II, the main powers allied against the Axis—Great Britain, the Soviet Union, China, and the United States.

apprentice someone who works for a qualified person to learn a trade.

Aryans in Nazi terms, a supposed "master race" of white people of non-Jewish descent, particularly with blond hair and blue eyes; most non-Aryans did not fit this description.

bankruptcy describes the state of being bankrupt, when a person or an organization is unable to pay debts.

Buddhists followers of Buddhism, a religion founded by Siddhartha Gautama (c.563–c.483 B.C.); Buddhists believe that the suffering in life can be overcome by mental and moral self-purification practices.

capitalism an economic system based on private ownership of land and industry.

Cold War the term used to describe the state of hostility and tension between the two superpowers—the Soviet Union and the United States—that existed after World War II until the early 1990s.

communist one who believes in a political system that aims to create a society in which everyone is equal; one of its central principles is communal ownership of property.

concentration camp a prison camp where nonmilitary people are held and often killed or worked or starved to death.

denomination a particular group within a religious faith.

Germanic relating to or coming from the area that is modern-day Germany.

Hanseatic League an association of towns formed in the fourteenth century to protect and control trade in northern Germany.

Hindus people who follow Hinduism, a religion of India in which God takes the form of many gods and goddesses; Hindus believe that a person is reborn many times.

Holocaust huge destruction and loss of life; when capitalized, the term is used to describe the mass killings of Jews and other groups considered undesirable by the Nazis during World War II.

Holy Roman Empire a collection of European territories that were all ruled by a Frankish or Germanic king from A.D. 800 to 1806.

Huguenots French Protestants who followed the teachings of John Calvin, persecuted by the Catholic government of France.

infrastructure the system of public works, such as water, roads, and electricity, in a region.

Reichstag the German parliament building.

reunification the act of joining together again; in Germany, it refers to the reuniting of East and West Germany.

Romanticism relating to the Romantic movement, an eighteenth- and early

Glossary

nineteenth-century European movement in art, literature, and music that emphasized feeling and free expression.

Salons meetings of artists, writers, scientists, or other notable people at the home of someone famous or important.

Saxon a people originally from the area of West Germany.

Secession the name taken by several groups of painters who broke away from traditional

styles of art and organized their own exhibitions of more experimental works.

Slavic describes people who came originally from the area of the Ukraine and Poland.

Stone Age the name given to a period in history when humans learned to use stone tools; it began about 2.5 million years ago and ended roughly in 3000 B.C.

subsidies amounts of money paid to help support a particular system or organization.

Further Information

Books

Bachrach, Susan D. *The Nazi Olympics, Berlin 1936.* Sagebrush Bound, 2001.

Dahlberg, Maurine F. *Escape to West Berlin.* Farrar, Straus and Giroux, 2004.

Hatt, Christine. *Berlin (World Cities).* Thameside Press, 1999.

Levy, Debbie. *The Berlin Wall (Building World Landmarks).* Blackbirch Press, 2004.

Smith, Jeremy. *The Fall of the Berlin Wall (Days That Changed the World).* World Almanac Library, 2004.

Stein, Richard Conrad. *Berlin.* Scholastic Library Publishing, 1997.

Web sites

www.dailysoft.com/berlinwall
See photographs, look at maps, and explore the history of the Berlin wall at this Web site.

www.dieberlinermauer.de
See images of life on either side of the Berlin Wall on this photographer's Web site.

www.newseum.org/berlinwall
This interactive Web site explores the news and how it was presented differently in East and West Berlin.

www.odci.gov/cia/publications/factbook/geos/gm.html
For a map and facts on Germany, check out the World Factbook site.

www.wall-berlin.org
Click on the British/United States flag for a virtual tour in English of the exhibit "A Concrete Curtain: The Life and Death of the Berlin Wall."

Index